BEETHOVEN
EGMONT
OVERTURE · OP. 84

OOSEY & HAWKES

No. 121

DATE DUE

Faculty			
GAYLORD			PRINTED IN U.S.A.

BEETHOVEN
EGMONT

OVERTURE
OP. 84

60¢

BOOSEY & HAWKES

LONDON   NEW YORK   SYDNEY   TORONTO   CAPETOWN

Litho'd in U. S. A.

EGMONT OVERTURE
OP. 84

In 1810, Beethoven composed the incidental music to Goethe's tragedy " Egmont ": Overture, two Songs, March and a " Symphony of Victory " accompanying Egmont's vision in prison of the final triumph of freedom over tyranny and oppression. Goethe's tragedy with Beethoven's music was first performed in Vienna, on May 24th, 1810. The main part of the " Symphony of Victory " forms the Coda of the overture which, otherwise, is independent of the incidental music.

EGMONT

OVERTURE

Sostenuto ma non troppo

L. van Beethoven, Op. 84
(1770-1827)

B. & H. 8443

2

B. & H. 8443

3

B. & H. 8443

5

B. & H. 8443

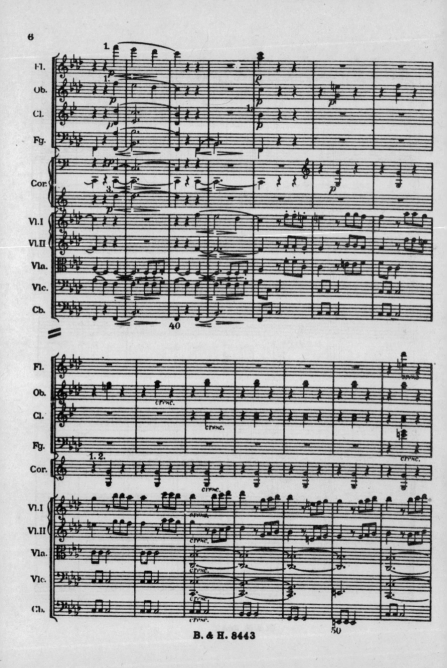

8

B. & H. 8443

10

B. & H. 8443

11

12

13

B. & H. 8443

14

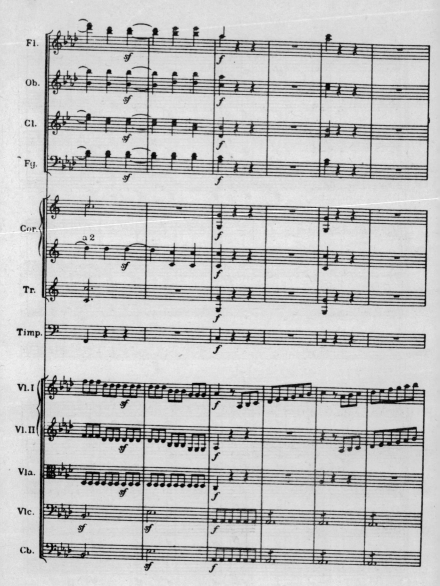

18

120

130

B. & H. 8443

17

140

B. & H. 8443

18

21

B. & H. 8443

24

26

28

30

B. & H. 8443

Flauto II muta in Flauto piccolo

290

34

B. & H. 8443

36

310

B. & H. 8443

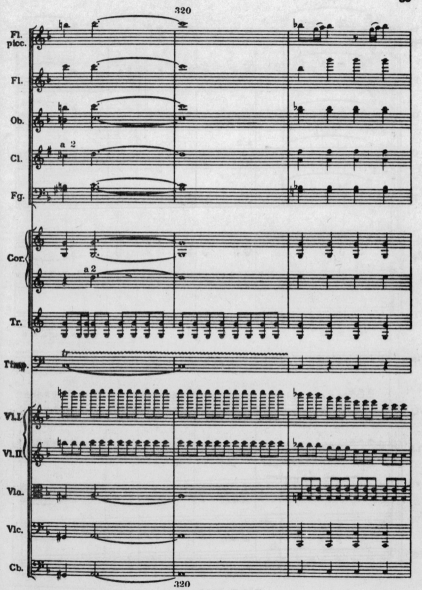

42

44